KEYS TO

VICTORIOUS

LIVING

FaithFamily Church

Formerly Canton Christian Fellowship

P.O. Box 35309
Canton, Ohio 44735
www.myfaithfamily.com
(888) 872-4991

Michael Cameneti

Tulsa, Oklahoma

KEYS TO VICTORIOUS LIVING

Keys to Victorious Living by Michael Cameneti
Published by Insight Publishing Group
8801 S. Yale, Suite 410
Tulsa, OK 74137
918-493-1718

Unless otherwise noted, all Scripture quotations are taken from *The Holy Bible, New King James Version*, (Nashville, Tennessee: Thomas Nelson, Inc.) 1982. Scriptures marked KJV are taken from *The King James Version*, (Cambridge: Cambridge) 1769. Scriptures marked NLT are taken from the *Holy Bible, New Living Translation*, (Wheaton, IL: Tyndale House Publishers, Inc.) 1996. Scriptures marked AMP are taken from *The Amplified Bible*, (Zondervan Bible Publishers, Grand Rapids, Michigan) 1985. Scriptures marked NIV are taken from the *New International Version* (International Bible Society, East Brunswick, N.J.) 1984

ISBN 1-930027-98-2
Library of Congress catalog card number: 2003102789

Printed in the United States of America

Dedication

I dedicate this book to my wonderful wife and my two children. Barb, you are my best friend, and I love you more and more every day. Michael and Stephanie, I love you both. You are both a blessing, and I am proud of all that you are doing in life.

Contents

Thank You

I want to thank Wendy Lazor and my wife, Barb, who took this book to the next level. Thank you for the endless hours of hard work.

Endorsements

I was extremely proud and blessed as I read Pastor Mike's manuscript for his newest book, *Keys to Victorious Living*! Proud because Pastor Mike is my brother and he and Barb faithfully served Gina and I as our outreach and youth pastors for four and a half years, blessed because this book fed me and opened my eyes further to the incredible freedom and authority that Jesus gave us through His death, burial, and resurrection and how to walk in it.

Pastor Mike did a masterful job teaching us about the seven keys we need to understand in order to walk in victory! I know all that read this book will be brought up to a higher level spiritually and begin to walk in a greater level of victory as they implement these Bible truths!

Joseph Cameneti
Senior Pastor, Believers' Christian Fellowship
Warren, Ohio

While many have heard the victorious gospel message, not all have been able to apply it to their everyday lives. Jesus made an important statement while He walked on the earth. He said, *"take heed therefore how ye hear: for whosoever hath, to him shall be given; and whosoever hath not, from him shall be taken even that which he seemeth to have"* (Luke 8:18).

Jesus made it clear that it is possible to hear, yet not hear. In other words we can hear with natural ears, yet miss what the Spirit of God is saying. Hearing the correct way will lead to understanding and understanding leads to application.

My brother, Pastor Michael Cameneti, has outlined for us practical keys essential to a victorious life. From the first to the last key, each insight can first of all be understood and secondly applied to everyday living.

May the abundant life of Jesus increase as you hear.

Tony Cameneti
President, Cameneti Ministries
Director, RHEMA Bible Training Center Singapore
Singapore

When I read Pastor Michael Cameneti's book, *Keys to Victorious Living,* my first thought was that this book should be required reading for every new believer. The truths in this book will make a huge impact in the life of every young Christian who reads and applies them. I can see people becoming solidly grounded in the faith as they learn these powerful keys, and experiencing acceleration and advancement in their spiritual growth as a result of their exposure to these principles.

My second impression was that this book will not simply benefit young believers. These are truths that even the most mature believer should be reminded of again and again! We not only need to experience spiritual growth as a baby Christian, but we need to be continually nourished as we move into maturity. I believe *Keys to Victorious Living* provides excellent nourishment regardless of the spiritual maturity level of the reader.

Pastor Mike is a very personable and excellent communicator. His message is full of rich, biblical insights and common sense, and he conveys great truths in a down-to-earth, easy-to-grasp way. I have no doubt that God's grace and his many years in pastoral ministry have made him skilled and adept in speaking to people in a very impacting way, and touching them "right where they live."

Get ready to embark on a great adventure! Read with an open and hungry heart! God will speak to you and strengthen your life as you read *Keys to Victorious Living*.

Tony Cooke
President, Tony Cooke Ministries
Tulsa, Oklahoma

Introduction

Having ministered for many years to many different people, my wife and I, as well as our staff, recognize the significant need people have for teaching taken directly from the Word of God. The power to receive all that God has provided for us and to live victoriously comes directly from His Word, and I believe that God intends that victory for all those who call on His name to be saved.

Jesus says in Matthew 16:19, *"And I will give you the keys of the kingdom of heaven, and whatever you bind on earth will be bound in heaven, and whatever you loose on earth will be loosed in heaven."* Jesus is telling us that the keys He gives us are the means by which we experience victory!

Keys represent entrance. For example, if I gave you the keys to my home, you would have the authority to enter my home—giving you access to anything inside. But keys also represent power and authority. If I gave you the keys to my car, you would have the authority and power to start my car and drive off. Knowing this, we can see that the keys of the kingdom of heaven give us the power and authority to access and utilize what God has provided for us.

When I first began writing this book, I considered listing salvation as the most important key to victorious living, because it is indeed, the first step—it gives you entrance into the kingdom of God. But I felt led to minister to those who already had a relationship with Christ—those who were already born again. This book is written from that perspective.

Second Corinthians 2:14 says, *"Now thanks be to God, who always leads us in triumph in Christ, and through us diffuses the fragrance of His knowledge in every place."* God is a victorious God, and He wants us to be His victorious sons and daughters!

And notice Ephesians 2:4-6 which says,

> *But God, who is rich in mercy, because of His great love with which He loved us, even when we were dead in trespasses, made us alive together with Christ (by grace you have been saved), and raised us up together, and made us sit together in the heavenly places in Christ Jesus.*

As believers, God makes us to sit in heavenly places together with Him. That's a place of victory. That's a platform for victory, and if you operate from that platform, you'll have victory in your life.

It's my heart to see the Church rise up to be the glorious, victorious Church God designed. As a pastor, I have seen believers who live their lives defeated in one area or another. There are some who struggle in the area of their relationships. For others, it is their finances. Many battle against sickness and disease, and for others, fear. God wants you to be an overcomer in this world. He doesn't want circumstances to defeat you!

Throughout this book, you will find tools—keys to victorious living—that will help you walk in victory. The foundation for every key is the Word of God; without it, you cannot access all that God has for you.

The blessings and benefits of God are endless. We couldn't possibly cover all of them in this book, but we will cover seven keys that I believe are necessary to help you become the victorious Christian God intends for you to be. It is my prayer that God will help you understand and apply the wonderful revelations of His plan for you, so you may enjoy the victorious life He wants for you!

Revelation Knowledge

As believers, we understand that salvation gives us entrance to the Kingdom of God. We also know that the Word is our guidebook, the most important tool we have for receiving and understanding the keys the Lord has provided, but without revelation knowledge we're limited. Why? Because revelation makes the Word of God come alive to you!

Let's talk about the word "revelation" before we look at some scriptures. The word "revelation" comes from the Greek word *apokalupsis*, and its meaning pertains to having a curtain that cuts off your view and then having it suddenly opened, revealing whatever is beyond.

> **Revelation makes the Word of God come alive to you!**

Let me give you an example. I was studying the Word and reading 1 Corinthians 7:3, where it says we're to show due benevolence to one another. And though I had read it before, I did so without truly understanding what it meant. While studying this time, however, it seemed to jump off the page at me. I received revelation on the subject—it became real to me, and I understood its true meaning! I discovered that "due benevolence" means "grace thinking," and that the Bible says we are to show it to one another.

At that moment, I realized what showing due benevolence to my wife would be like. Understand, before I received revelation on the subject I *used* to think that when my wife treated me a certain way, I'd do the same for her. But having received revelation about it, I realized that if I showed due benevolence to her, I'd treat her with grace whether or not she earned it or returned it. It was a revelation that stopped me from simply reading about it and caused me to actually *act upon it*. It changed our relationship.

That is why revelation knowledge is one of the most important keys to victorious living. Revelation makes the Word of God come alive to you! The affect of that happening will change your life. You'll see the power of the Word of God!

The Light of Revelation

Let me describe another example of revelation. Imagine you are hungry and in need of something to eat. You're in a dark kitchen; the lights are off, and you can't see. However, when you open the refrigerator, the light comes on and, all of a sudden you can see! You've been starving in a dark room, but as you open the door, the light comes on and you can finally see the food that's been in the room with you all along. What happened? Well, when the light came on, you saw what you had available to you.

As believers, we've been born again. God lives in us, and there's an incorruptible seed in us, but we can still walk in darkness in certain areas of our lives. Why? One reason may be that the light hasn't come on yet. We can't see the provision of God that is right there before us. The refrigerator is there, the food is inside, but the door is closed and the light's off. You can be a believer yet still walk in defeat because the light hasn't come on in your own personal life.

You might say, "Well it can't be off. I'm a believer." No, even though you've heard all the sermons, you can still be living without victory. Even though you prayed the prayer of salvation, you can be standing in front of the unlocked refrigerator of the Kingdom and yet be slowly starving just an arm's length away from food. The provision is there, but until the light comes on, you can't see it.

Here's a great thing about revelation. When the light comes on in your life, you can see what the Word says to *you*, and when it becomes real to you, no one can shake you from it. God has put it in your heart! The light is on, you can see the blessings, and you can partake of them.

Revelation for Salvation

John 3:16 says, *"For God so loved the world that He gave His only begotten Son, that whoever believes in Him should not perish but have everlasting life."* And Romans 10: 9,10 tells us that provision for all men to be saved has already been done through Jesus. He has paid the price for all men to be saved.

But let me ask you this question: when does a person get saved? It begins when he *sees the truth of salvation available to him*. Once he sees, he can act on the revelation knowledge he now has, and call on the name of the Lord. Many people haven't yet called on His name because they haven't *seen* the truth!

When I saw that I was a sinner, that I needed a Savior, and that I had to confess Jesus as Lord, everything changed. Yes, each person has a different experience with salvation—some lives are radically changed instantly while others are more of a gradual change—but one fact remains the same for every believer. We saw the need for Jesus in our lives.

I received Jesus while listening to a radio broadcast. I was in my car, coming home from work at nine o'clock at night. I was flipping through stations and the preacher said, "Don't touch that dial!" I thought, "Oh my God. God's speaking to me!" So I didn't touch the dial. As I pulled up my driveway, he said, "I want you to pray this prayer with me if you've never prayed it before."

So I said, "Father, I confess Jesus as Lord." I prayed the prayer with him and was changed in an instant! What happened? Well, revelation for salvation came. I believed it in my heart, I confessed it with my mouth; and I was saved.

How Does Revelation Come?

According to Ephesians 1:15-18, you need to ask God for revelation. It says,

> *Therefore I also, after I heard of your faith in the Lord Jesus and your love for all the saints, do not cease to give thanks for you, making mention of you in my prayers:*

that the God of our Lord Jesus Christ, the Father of glory, may give to you the spirit of wisdom and revelation in the knowledge of Him, the eyes of your understanding being enlightened; that you may know what is the hope of His calling.

Notice how Paul prayed for the church in Ephesus, *"That the God of our Lord Jesus Christ, the Father of glory, may give to you the spirit of wisdom and revelation in the knowledge of Him, the eyes of your understanding being enlightened."*

He's praying for the Spirit of wisdom and *revelation in the knowledge of God* to come to them. Notice that knowledge is a very important component. When you read the Bible, or hear the Word through your pastor and other ministry gifts,

> Paul prayed that their spiritual eyes would be enlightened.

you're gaining knowledge of the things of God. That knowledge is what God takes and uses as you pray for wisdom and revelation. He will take what you've learned and make it real to you—you'll receive personal revelation. That is why it is so important to be in church, to hear the Word, and to meditate on scriptures.

So what did Paul mean when he prayed that the eyes of their understanding would be enlightened? We have two sets of eyes. The natural ones enable us see the things of this world. The spiritual eyes enable us to see (or understand) the things of God. Paul prayed that their spiritual eyes would be enlightened—that the light would come on! Paul understood that there could be times where, even though you're saved, there is still a form of darkness in your life—a lack of illumination and understanding.

You need to start asking God, "God open up my eyes. Flood me with light."

We have a man in our church that came up to me once and told me that the Bible promises weren't working for him. We talked about it for a moment, and I discovered that he wasn't experiencing the prosperity he thought he should be. He agreed to go home and lock himself in his prayer closet until God answered a question for him regarding why he was in the condition he was. He prayed, asking God to open up the eyes of his heart, and all of a sudden, God gave him an invention. Now he's become a very blessed man.

The answer here isn't for all people with financial problems to expect to invent something. The answer is seeking God and asking Him for the eyes of your understanding to be opened. He may deal with you about being a better steward with your money. Or He may deal with you concerning tithing and giving offerings. Whatever it is He shows you, be obedient to do what He tells you to do. When you receive revelation knowledge of how you are to respond, do it.

It's unfortunate. Many believers are in the condition they are in because they have not gone to God and asked for revelation. They want all the blessings and benefits of God, but they don't want to spend time in prayer asking God to open their eyes. And, others simply choose not to obey the revelation knowledge He gives. God still loves them, He just can't operate at the level He'd like to in their lives. If you're in that position, I have good news for you—God's mercies are new every morning (Lamentations 3:22,23)! Make the adjustment and get back on track.

If you are hungry for revelation in your life, pray every day for God to give you a Spirit of wisdom and revelation in the knowledge of Him, that He would open the eyes of your understanding. Ask God to give you revelation, the key that unlocks the Word to you, making it real in your daily life. He wants our eyes to be opened. He wants us to see His goodness, His power, His ability, His plan!

What Revelation Knowledge Do You Need?

There are many things the Bible instructs us to pray for regarding revelation. As we read on in Ephesians, we see three things that Paul specifically prays will dawn on the hearts of believers. In Ephesians 1:18,19, Paul prays, *"that you may know what is the hope of His calling, what are the riches of the glory of His inheritance in the saints, and what is the exceeding greatness of His power toward us who believe."*

- The first part of Paul's prayer is that they may know the hope of His calling.
- The second is that they'll understand the riches of the glory of His inheritance in the saints.
- The last is that they will comprehend the exceeding greatness of His power toward them.

Key Nugget: Know His Calling in Your Life

Although not all of us are called to ministry, every person has a God-ordained purpose in life. You *need* to know your calling. When God reveals your calling to you, it changes everything. When you know your calling, it gives you purpose. When you have purpose, it drives you. And when you're driven, you never have to ask yourself why you're here, what you're doing, or why you're doing it—you *know*. You have the revelation of the wonderful future God has for you. He wants to give you that drive, that purpose, no matter how young or old you are.

Notice what Paul wrote to the believers at Colosse in Colossians 1:9,10,

> *For this reason we also, since the day we heard it, do not cease to pray for you, and to ask that you may be filled with the knowledge of His will in all wisdom and spiritual understanding; that you may walk worthy of the Lord, fully pleasing Him, being fruitful in every good work and increasing in the knowledge of God.*

Paul heard of their salvation, and he prayed as Elijah did when he prayed about rain—effectively and fervently. (See James 5:16-18.) Paul knew how to pray in accordance with the will of God, and he prayed that they would be *filled* with the knowledge of His will.

The word "filled," *pleroo* in the Greek language, means, "to cram or to stuff." Paul prayed that they would have knowledge of God's will, and that they might be crammed and stuffed with it. And we can pray that way, too. Think about that!

A person who works a job not knowing if he's where God called him to be will always be looking for another place. Why? Because when you don't know the will of God for your life, you'll never be satisfied. The same can be said for people who enter into a relationship.

A person who isn't stuffed with the knowledge of God's will, often looks for other ways to fill his life. See, when you know the will of God for your life—when you're crammed and stuffed with it—you're not going to look for other things.

Consider this illustration. My mother makes the best Italian dinners, so when Christmas comes around I load everything on my plate three times! I'm often so stuffed that all I can do is lie on the floor with my feet up, watching TV and moaning. I always tell myself I'll never do it again, but the next year comes around, and I do it once more. Hopefully you can identify with me in being so stuffed that you're uncomfortable and couldn't possibly eat another bite.

What would your life be like if you were so stuffed with God that you couldn't eat another bite of anything else? If you were crammed with the knowledge of God's will, what would happen? No one and no thing could get you off track—no person and no devil could dissuade your direction. You would know what the will of God is for your life, and what God has called you to do. Then the devil could tempt and try to distract you with anything else, and you'd say, "Absolutely not. I'm stuffed—not another bite." Why? Because you're crammed with God's will for you. You live it. You breathe it. It's stuffed on the inside of you, and there is no room for anything else.

Many Christians are frustrated because they are looking to other things to fill and satisfy their lives; and they will always be hungry until they get crammed full of God's will for them. They need to pray and seek His will through revelation.

Key Nugget: Know Your Inheritance

You don't get an inheritance until someone dies. In the same way, Hebrews 9:15-17 tells us that for the new covenant to begin, there had to be a death; Jesus had to die. And when Jesus died *and* rose from the dead, He gave you an inheritance!

There's an earthly side and there's a heavenly side to our inheritance. Your heavenly inheritance includes a place that Jesus has gone ahead to prepare for you—a mansion in heaven with His Father, a redeemed body, and crowns and rewards. All of that is

> **When Jesus died *and* rose from the dead, He gave you an inheritance.**

wonderful, and I look forward to it with a sense of great expectation, but there are also things I need daily while on this earth. That's where our earthly inheritance comes in.

Paul's prayer for the Ephesians involves your earthly inheritance, which you can have *today*. Paul is praying that the eyes of their understanding would be enlightened, the eyes of their hearts would be opened and flooded with light, that they can have revelations as to their earthly inheritance—our earthly inheritance.

What Is Our Earthly Inheritance?

God has provided us with an abundance of blessings and benefits as part of our earthly inheritance! Here are some of them:

◆ **The Holy Ghost lives inside you**—(John 14:16; Ephesians 1:13)

- ◆ **The armor of God**—(Ephesians 6:11-13; 2 Corinthians 6:7)
- ◆ **Healing**—(1 Peter 2:24; Matthew 8:17)
- ◆ **Prosperity**—(2 Corinthians 8:9; 3 John 3)
- ◆ **Faith**—(Romans 12:3; 2 Peter 1:1)
- ◆ **Peace**—(John 14:27; Philippians 4:7)
- ◆ **Fruit of the Spirit**—(Galatians 5:22,23; 2 Corinthians 6:3-6)

All of these things are provided at the time you accept Jesus and become a believer. However, Paul prays for the eyes of their understanding to be opened. This indicates to me that we need to pray that our spiritual eyes may be open so that we can see and understand this inheritance. You may have all of these wonderful blessings as your inheritance, but if you don't know about them, they won't help you walk in victory in your life.

When I have *revelation* that the love of God is shed abroad in my heart, as it says in Romans 5:5, that is when I can truly love people who seem unlovable, and I can love people who treat me poorly. When I have *revelation* of the healing Christ provided by His death on the cross, I won't allow sickness to reign in my body. When I have *revelation* that God will supply all my needs according to His riches in glory, and I understand that poverty is not part of my inheritance, I can reject poverty in my life.

The Bible says that Jesus became poor so that we could be made rich; He took sickness on Himself so that we could experience health; He paid the price for sin so that we could have eternal life. Wow! What an inheritance! We have both a heavenly and an earthly inheritance, and while the heavenly one is a wonderful expectation for eternity, we have the earthly inheritance to enjoy today.

Praying for Others

By now, you should begin to see that prayer is intimately involved in your receiving revelation in your own life, but did you know that we can pray for others—that they would receive revelation—just as Paul prayed for the Ephesians?

When I first got saved I used to pray for others and at times my prayers went something like this, "God, I'm so tired of him. If you don't change him, I will." Have you ever done that? Sometimes we pray for our spouse or other loved ones and say, "Lord, just change them! They're mean and unruly, and You need to change them!"

But God moves on heartfelt prayers that line up with His Word. When we pray, "Father open up the eyes of their hearts; not the way I want them opened, not for them to see what I want them to see, but Lord flood them with light, and give them knowledge of Your Word and Your will," we're praying in line with the Word of God! When I received revelation of that fact, I began praying for others, "Father, open up their eyes. Give them a spirit of wisdom and revelation. Flood them with light on the inner man."

First Corinthians 2:9 says, "*But as it is written: Eye has not seen, nor ear heard, nor have entered into the heart of man the things which God has prepared for those who love Him.*" What God has prepared for some people has not entered into their hearts yet. When it does, change will come. That person who frustrates you, that family member who irritates you, that child who aggravates you, that mate who infuriates you—when revelation enters into their hearts, that's when they'll change.

Why Revelation Doesn't Come

Let's take a moment to look at why revelation *doesn't* come. Some people can sit through countless services, and yet they never seem to have revelation enter their hearts. The traditions of men—holding what man says more dearly than what God says—can halt revelation in a person's life. It's important not to substitute traditional beliefs for what is *really* in the Bible, and we need to evaluate our practices against the Word frequently.

Another reason is religion. Religion is different from tradition; traditions are just hard-held beliefs, but religion is legalistic ceremony. How did Jesus handle religious people? In John 8:44 He went up to them and said, *"You are of your father, the devil."* Jesus despised the religious rules that the Jews had trapped themselves with—the rules that kept them from seeing Him as

> **Jesus didn't come to bring more rules; He came to bring completion to the Law.**

the Messiah. Jesus didn't come to bring more rules; He came to bring completion to the Law, and put us over into love and revelation so that we can walk in victory.

Notice 1 Corinthians 2:9-12,

> *But as it is written: "Eye has not seen, nor ear heard, nor have entered into the heart of man the things which God has prepared for those who love Him." But God has revealed them to us through His Spirit. For the Spirit searches all things, yes, the deep things of God. For what man knows the things of a man except the*

spirit of the man which is in him? Even so no one knows the things of God except the Spirit of God. Now we have received, not the spirit of the world, but the Spirit who is from God, that we might know the things that have been freely given to us by God.

Notice what it says in verse 10: *"God has revealed them [the things that God has prepared for those who love Him] to us through His Spirit."* That is how revelation comes—by the Spirit of God. In the New Living Translation, verse 11 says, *"No one can know what anyone else is really thinking except that person alone, and no one can know God's thoughts except God's own Spirit."* No one knows what's going on inside another person's heart or head but that person—and God. Men don't know God's thoughts except by His Holy Spirit. Look at verse 12 again, *"Now we have received, not the spirit of the world, but the Spirit who is from God, that we might know the things that have been freely given to us by God."* The New Living says, *"And God has actually given us his Spirit (not the world's spirit) so we can know the wonderful things God has freely given us."*

This scripture is telling us that the things God has prepared for you are beyond your imagination, but He will reveal them to you through His Spirit—the same Spirit that knows His thoughts and heart as surely as our own spirit knows our thoughts and heart.

God wants to remove obstacles that block our understanding and openness to His revelation. He wants us to be free of the traditions of men and religious preconceptions that keep us from receiving what He wants to give.

In Acts 19, Paul is preaching and asks if they have received the Holy Ghost. They say, "We haven't heard that there's such a thing as the Holy Ghost." Although they had no knowledge of the Holy Ghost, they had nothing holding them back from receiving the revelation. They didn't have traditions of man that said the gift of tongues is dead or that prophecy has ceased. They didn't have religious conventions that kept them bound by legalism and regulations.

Fervent prayer for yourself and others will bring revelation, and as you receive revelation, God fills you with an understanding of His will. Prayer is vital! Prayer will open the door of revelation for your life, and when you are stuffed with the knowledge of God's will for your life, there will be no room for distractions, no room for poverty, no room for sickness, and no room for the devil's deception. He won't be able to turn you from your course and keep you from living victoriously!

Key # 2

The Role of the Holy Spirit

In the previous chapter, we talked about revelation—God unveiling His Word and His Will to you so that it becomes real in your heart. The second key to victorious living that we're going to cover is acknowledging the role of the Holy Spirit in your life. Notice what Jesus says about the Holy Spirit in John 14:16 (AMP): *"And I will ask the Father, and He will give you another Comforter (Counselor, Helper, Intercessor, Advocate, Strengthener, and Standby), that He may remain with you forever."* The Greek literally says that He will make His permanent house on the inside of you.

Notice what Jesus goes on to say in John 16:13,14, (AMP):

> But when He, the Spirit of Truth (the Truth-giving Spirit) comes, He will guide you into all the Truth (the whole, full Truth). For He will not speak His own

message [on His own authority]; but He will tell what-
ever He hears [from the Father; He will give the message
that has been given to Him], and He will announce and
declare to you the things that are to come [that will
happen in the future]. He will honor and glorify Me,
because He will take of (receive, draw upon) what is Mine
and will reveal (declare, disclose, transmit) it to you.

This passage of Scripture should be enough for you
to realize that the role of the Holy Spirit is to help you live
a life of victory! But what many believers don't understand
is that they have a part to play
in this. If you want to experience the fullness of the benefits of the Holy Spirit that we
just read about, then you need

> **The role of the Holy Spirit is to help you live a life of victory.**

to be baptized in the Holy Spirit with the evidence of
speaking in other tongues, and you need to learn how to be
led by the Spirit.

Baptism of the Holy Spirit

When you are born again, the Holy Spirit comes to
dwell on the inside of you—there is no doubt about that.
But being baptized in the Holy Spirit—filled with the
Holy Spirit—is a completely different experience that
follows salvation.

Notice the account of the Day of Pentecost. In Acts
1:5 Jesus told the apostles that they would be *"baptized*
with the Holy Spirit not many days from now." So after Jesus
ascended into Heaven, the apostles assembled together
and on the Day of Pentecost they were filled with the

Holy Ghost and began to speak in tongues as the Spirit gave them utterance (Acts 2:1-4). They were baptized in the Holy Spirit!

Let's look at another example, found in Acts 19:1-6, where the Apostle Paul speaks to a group of believers at Ephesus:

> *And it happened, while Apollos was at Corinth, that Paul, having passed through the upper regions, came to Ephesus. And finding some disciples he said to them,* **"Did you receive the Holy Spirit when you believed***?" So they said to him, "We have not so much as heard whether there is a Holy Spirit." And he said to them, "Into what then were you baptized?" So they said, "Into John's baptism." Then Paul said, "John indeed baptized with a baptism of repentance, saying to the people that they should believe on Him who would come after him, that is, on Christ Jesus." When they heard this, they were baptized in the name of the Lord Jesus. And when Paul had laid hands on them, the Holy Spirit came upon them, and they spoke with tongues and prophesied.* (Emphasis added)

It's important to notice that Paul asked them *"Did you receive the Holy Spirit when you believed?"* Again, that shows us that there is another experience aside from the Holy Ghost coming to dwell on the inside of us when we are born again. And notice what took place after they were baptized in the Name of Jesus: Paul laid his hands upon them, the Holy Ghost came on them, and they spoke with other tongues. They were baptized in the Holy Spirit!

Historians estimate that this account at Ephesus took place thirty-five to forty years after the Day of Pentecost, and this is just one example of many. That shows us that the baptism of the Holy Spirit with the evidence of speaking in other tongues isn't exclusive to those present at the Day of Pentecost. Being Spirit filled is meant for every believer, including us today!

Now that you understand that the Baptism of the Holy Spirit is another experience aside from salvation, I want to look at these examples again, because there is something else I want you to see. Jesus told the apostles not to depart from Jerusalem until they had received the promise of the Holy Spirit (Acts 1:4). Why was it so important that they wait? Notice what Jesus says in Acts 1:8, *"But you shall receive power when the Holy Spirit has come upon you."* The apostles would receive power when they were baptized in the Holy Spirit!

> **Being Spirit filled is meant for every believer, including us today!**

Now I want to focus on the fact that Paul felt it was necessary to make sure the believers in Ephesus received the baptism of the Holy Spirit. Not only did he ask them if they had received the Holy Ghost (Acts 19:2), but he made sure they did (Acts 19:6)! Why? He was aware of the power they would receive as a result. He understood the benefits of praying in tongues.

Benefits of Praying in Tongues

Speaking in tongues is the evidence of the Baptism of the Holy Spirit, and it is something you should do on a regular basis. Praying in tongues (praying in the Spirit) is not a natural thing; it's supernatural. And the benefits of praying in tongues are powerful and unmatched by anything you can do on your own.

When you pray in your understanding, your prayers are limited to what *you* know. When you pray in tongues, you yield your tongue to the Holy Spirit and *He* directs your prayers!

◆ When you pray in tongues, you edify yourself; you build yourself up. Notice 1 Corinthians 14:4, which says, *"He who speaks in a tongue edifies himself, but he who prophesies edifies the church."*

This scripture in the Greek says that it will "build a megastructure on the inside of you." What does that mean? When you pray in tongues, you stir up the gift of the Holy Spirit on the inside of you (2 Timothy 1:6), you are strengthened in your inner man—you're filled up with God.

◆ Another benefit of praying in tongues is that the Holy Spirit helps your limitations. Romans 8:26 tells us, *"Likewise the Spirit also helps in our weaknesses. For we do not know what we should pray for as we ought, but the Spirit Himself makes intercession for us with groanings which cannot be uttered."*

Have you ever faced a situation not knowing what or how to pray? That's exactly what this scripture is talking about. You may not know everything there is to know about that situation, but the Holy

Spirit does. So as you pray in tongues, you can trust that the perfect prayer—prayer that is in line with the perfect will of God—will come forth.

◆ Praying in tongues is also a way to strengthen or build your faith. Notice Jude 20, which says, *"But you, beloved, building yourselves up on your most holy faith, praying in the Holy Spirit."*

The Bible says that faith will come into your life by the Word of God (Romans 10:17), and the word "build" in Jude 20 in the Greek language means to "build upon something that already exists." As you put the Word of God into your life and pray in tongues, you'll build upon what already exists on the inside of you. You'll build your faith.

◆ Praying in tongues is a way to magnify God. Look at Acts 10:46, which says, *"For they heard them speak with tongues, and magnify God."*

When you pray in tongues and magnify God, you begin to see Him for who He is—Almighty God, Creator of the heavens and the earth. Understand, however, you're not making God any bigger than He already is—He's God. But you are making Him bigger in your own eyes. When that happens, problems no longer overwhelm you because your attention is focused on how big God is, not how big your problem is.

◆ You can be refreshed by praying in tongues. Isaiah 28:11,12 says, *"For with stammering lips and another tongue will he speak to this people. To whom he said, 'This is the rest with which you may cause the weary to rest; and this is the refreshing:' yet they would not hear."*

If you've ever hit a point where you feel as if you are spiritually drained, praying in tongues will refresh you. That's what this scripture is referring to.

◆ Praying in tongues is a way to give thanks to God well. Notice 1 Corinthians 14:15-17 where Paul writes,

What is the conclusion then? I will pray with the spirit, and I will also pray with the understanding. I will sing with the spirit, and I will also sing with the understanding. Otherwise, if you bless with the spirit, how will he who occupies the place of the uninformed say "Amen" at your giving of thanks, since he does not understand what you say? For you indeed give thanks well, but the other is not edified.

Have you ever felt as if you can't find enough words to express to God how good He is and how thankful you are to Him? Paul is telling us here that by praying in tongues we can give thanks to God well.

◆ You can pray out mysteries and secrets when you pray in tongues. Look at 1 Corinthians 14:2, which says, *"For he who speaks in a tongue does not speak to men but to God, for no one understands him; however, in the spirit he speaks mysteries."*

When you pray in tongues you can be praying out the path your career will take, who you are supposed to marry, and so forth. You can pray about your future! Remember what we read in John 16:13 at the beginning of this chapter—the Holy Spirit will show you things to come. The Holy Spirit knows everything you're going to face and the plan of God for your life, so when you yield your tongue to Him, things get accomplished that you could never accomplish in the natural.

◆ Praying in tongues will help keep you from saying things that you probably shouldn't say. James 3:8-10 says, *"But no man can tame the tongue. It is an unruly evil, full of deadly poison. With it we bless our God and Father, and with it we curse men, who have been made in the similitude of God. Out of the same mouth proceed blessing and cursing. My brethren, these things ought not to be so."*

When you pray in tongues, it brings about a greater awareness of the fact that you've got the Holy Spirit living on the inside of you. So you'll choose your words carefully, not wanting to grieve the Holy Spirit.

◆ Praying in tongues will give you a greater revelation of God's abiding presence within you, and it keeps you under conviction to live a life that is right and in line with the Word of God. John 14:16,17 reads,

And I will pray the Father, and He will give you another Helper, that He may abide with you forever— the Spirit of truth, whom the world cannot receive, because it neither sees Him nor knows Him; but you know Him, for He dwells with you and will be in you.

There's something about acknowledging that the Holy Spirit lives on the inside of you that brings conviction to keep your heart right before God.

Knowing that all of these benefits come from praying in tongues, we can now understand why the Apostle Paul wrote in 1 Corinthians 14:18, *"I thank my God I speak with tongues more than you all."* He understood the importance of the Holy Spirit, and allowed Him to have an active role in his life. As a result, the New Testament is filled with examples of Paul's incredible victories!

Being Led by the Spirit

So we've established the importance of the Baptism of the Holy Spirit, and we've reviewed the benefits that come as a result of spending time praying in the Spirit. Now I want to show you the importance of learning how to be led by the Spirit.

Often we hear terms such as listening to the Spirit and being led by the Spirit, but without a revelation about the very real work of the Spirit in our lives, we often dismiss it as charismatic talk. As you study your Bible, you will see that the Holy Spirit is very real and can be a discernable voice inside of you daily.

We are three-part beings. In 1 Thessalonians 5:23, Paul, praying for the Thessalonians, says that he's praying for them spirit, soul, and body. He said, *"Now may the God of peace Himself sanctify you completely; and may your whole spirit, soul, and body be preserved blameless at the coming of our Lord Jesus Christ."*

> **The Holy Spirit is very real and can be a discernable voice inside of you daily.**

God Leads Your Spirit

You are a spirit-being who has a soul (or mind) and who lives in a body. John 4:24 says, *"God is Spirit, and those who worship Him must worship in spirit and truth."* God is also a Spirit, so it makes sense that He's going to talk to your spirit.

I've had many people tell me, "I don't know if the thought I had was God speaking to me, or if it was just me. I don't know if it was the devil. I don't know who it was!" People get all confused. As believers, we're not to be confused. The Bible is very clear that we can be led by His Spirit.

Romans 8:14 says, *"For as many as are led by the Spirit of God, these are sons of God."* It doesn't read quite that way in the Greek, because this almost makes it sound as though you are not really a son or daughter of God if you're not led. What it means is that if you are a son or daughter of God, His Spirit *will* lead you. Romans 8:15-17 goes on to say, *"For you did not receive the spirit of bondage again to fear, but you received the Spirit of adoption by whom we cry out, 'Abba, Father.' The Spirit Himself bears witness with our spirit that we are children of God, and if children, then heirs—heirs of God and joint heirs with Christ."*

You're to be led by the Spirit of God if you're a son or a daughter of God. So God *is* going to speak to your spirit.

The Spirit of God is always trying to lead you. He wants to lead you out of bad situations; He wants to lead you away from accidents. God is not in the business of laughing at our foolishness when we step into bad situations; His Spirit is trying to lead us away from them.

Many Voices

First Corinthians 14:10 (KJV) says, *"There are, it may be, so many kinds of voices in the world, and none of them is without signification."* This tells us that there are many voices in the world, and each of those voices has significance.

This is yet another reason why it is so important to carefully choose your friends, the church you attend, and the ministry tapes you listen to—because they are going to speak into your life. What kind of voices are there in your life, and what are they saying to you? Does what they say make you doubt that God heals? Do they tell you that He doesn't prosper you? Or do they encourage you with the Word? There are many voices in the world. Each one of them will influence you in one way or another.

The Way God Speaks

God *can* speak to you in an audible voice. That will not be the norm, but He has, can, and does. There are also times in the book of Acts where people had visions and the Spirit of God spoke to them through the vision. Most of the time however, God will speak to you through His Holy Spirit to your spirit—through the still, small voice on the inside of you. Another way to describe that still small voice is that sometimes you just *know* something.

As Christians, we want to be led by the Lord, and many new Christians hear the familiar phrases we use in the Church—"I heard the Lord tell me to do this" or, "I heard the Lord tell me to do that"—and they get frustrated because they never *hear* anything. They often do not know that most Christians aren't hearing audible voices, but that they are simply referring to a knowing on the inside—that still small voice.

The Still, Small Voice

Acts 15:25-28 says,

It seemed good to us, *being assembled with one accord, to send chosen men to you with our beloved Barnabas and Paul, men who have risked their lives for the name of our Lord Jesus Christ.* (Emphasis added)

Notice how this works: The Bible says, "*It seemed good to us.*" There are times the Spirit just gives you something on the inside—it just seems right; you just know.

The Old Testament talks about God passing by Elijah. God wasn't in the fire; He wasn't in the earthquake; but He was in the still, small voice (1 Kings 19:11,12). Romans 8:16 says it this way: *"The Spirit Himself bears witness with our spirit that we are children of God."* In other words, the Holy Spirit gives confirmation (a knowing on the inside) to the things that are right and true.

In Romans 9:1 Paul says, *"I say the truth in Christ, I lie not, my conscience also bearing me witness in the Holy Ghost."* Our conscience is the voice or expression of the Spirit. The *witness* we're given is a spiritual sense—not a feeling, but a spiritual knowledge. Many times, being led by the Spirit is simply following that witness we have on the inside. It's a confirmation between our spirit and the Holy Spirit that leads us.

The Spirit Leads Us Through the Word

Jesus said in John 10:14-16,

I am the good shepherd; and I know My sheep, and am known by My own. As the Father knows Me, even so I know the Father; and I lay down My life for the sheep. And other sheep I have which are not of this fold; them also I must bring, and they will hear My voice; and there will be one flock and one shepherd.

Jesus said His sheep know His voice. As believers and children of God, we're not supposed to be confused regarding the voice of God in our lives. One of the ways you can ensure the leading you're receiving is from God is by being well founded in the written Word of God. God will never speak to you opposite of what His written Word says. 1 John 5:7 says, *"For there are three that bear witness in heaven: the Father, the Word, and the Holy Spirit; and these three are one."*

Once you start learning what the Word says, you'll be able to discern any voice that comes to you. You'll know when something is and is not of God, because the Spirit inside of you and the Word of God are one. If you want to know His voice, know the Word (John 1:1-3)!

Psalm 119:105 says, *"Your word is a lamp to my feet and a light to my path."* This is talking about The Word of God. Psalm 119:130 says, *"The entrance of Your words gives light; it gives understanding to the simple."* And then in Psalm 119:133, it says, *"Direct my steps by Your Word, and let no iniquity have dominion over me."* Learning God's Word sheds light on your situations and directs your steps. Remember what we learned in the previous chapter about revelation knowledge: If your eyes have not been enlightened, you need to pray like the Apostle Paul did in Ephesians chapter 1 and ask God to open the eyes of your understanding. Then, through the combination of the Word of God and the witness of the Holy Ghost, you can be led to make decisions that will help you live victoriously.

People say things like, "I don't know who I should marry." They don't understand that the answer can be found by feeding on the Word. The Word will show you what a godly woman is and what a godly man is; the Word will show you what to look for. Then God can speak to your heart and lead you by the inward witness.

Proverbs 20:27 says, *"The spirit of a man is the lamp of the Lord, searching all the inner depths of his heart."* The

Word is saying that God will enlighten you through and by His Spirit. We're not talking about just some light; we're talking about the Word of God *being* light. Jesus *is* light, and He enlightens you through your spirit. *He* lets you know what you need to do. *He* speaks to you as you put the Word of God in your heart.

Proverbs 6:22,23 says, talking about the Word, *"When you roam, they will lead you; When you sleep, they will keep you; And when you awake, they will speak with you. For the commandment is a lamp, and the law a light; reproofs of instruction are the way of life."* Now if the Word of God is the voice talking to you, it's a good thing. If you hear the Word in your head in the morning when you get out of bed, you're in a good place spiritually. If you're dwelling on the Word and it's continuing to speak to you as you go to bed, you're on the right track.

So, there are two main voices that lead us, as believers. They are the voice of the Word and the voice of the Spirit.

Judging Voices by the Word

The most important thing to understand when we talk about being led by the Spirit is that you must put the Word in you so that you can judge any voice by what the Word says. You must put any voice you hear up

> You must put the Word in you so that you can judge any voice by what the Word says.

against the Word and say, "What does the Word of God have to say?"

Now pay close attention: if something tells you to divorce your mate—unless there is something extreme such as abuse involved—you immediately know that can't be God. The Holy Ghost will never tell you to do something that doesn't line up with the Word of God. I've had people that have come up to me and say, "Pastor, the Lord told me to leave my spouse, and I'm supposed to marry this other person." I have told people like that, "That's not right; it's not in the Word." And you know what they told me? "I don't care about that. I heard a voice, and I'm going to do what I believe I was told to do."

Second Peter 1:19-21 says,

And so we have the prophetic word confirmed, which you do well to heed as a light that shines in a dark place, until the day dawns and the morning star rises in your hearts; knowing this first, that no prophecy of Scripture is of any private interpretation, for prophecy never came by the will of man, but holy men of God spoke as they were moved by the Holy Spirit.

Peter is not only referring to the written Word of God, but he's also making reference to the spoken Word of God. In verse 18 he talks about the event that occurred on the Mount of Transfiguration, *"And we heard this voice which came from heaven when we were with Him on the holy mountain."*

Peter heard a voice—audibly. Jesus was there, and Peter actually heard a voice—God's voice! He heard God speak and say, "This is my beloved Son, in Whom I am well pleased." But notice what Peter emphasizes in verses 19-21—as believers, we have an even more sure, more solid, more firm, and more stable Word. Peter, who heard the audible voice of God, is informing believers that the written Word of the Lord is more valuable than even this audible thunder that was the voice of the Lord. Wow!

What does that mean for believers? It means that the Bible is more valuable than any other voice. There is no voice or prophecy that supercedes the Word of God; if they don't match up, the Word is right and everything else is *wrong*.

When you get the Word in you, you can check to see if what someone says lines up with the Bible by comparing it to the Word that you've put inside you. The Bible, the Word of God, is the *surest* word of prophecy, and God never does anything that doesn't line up with His Word.

First Peter 1:23-25 says,

Having been born again, not of corruptible seed but incorruptible, through the word of God which lives and abides forever, because "All flesh is as grass, And all the glory of man as the flower of the grass. The grass withers, And its flower falls away, But the Word of the Lord endures forever." Now this is the word which by the gospel was preached to you.

If a voice came to you today and said, "The Lord wants you to die of cancer," you need to be able to say, "Absolutely not! He came to give me life and life more abundantly. It's the thief that comes to kill and destroy!" (John 10:10) You need to become familiar enough with what God says through His Word that when you hear a voice—whether inside you or coming through another person—you'll be able to discern from which spirit it comes. You'll know not to do something that you're told not to do in the Word, and you'll recognize the still, small voice of the Holy Ghost inside you when He begins to lead you and guide you.

You Must Learn to Hear

Let me remind you, we are talking about being led by the Spirit. But God cannot accurately lead you by the Spirit if you do not have the written Word as a foundation in your life. Instead of speaking to you through His Spirit in a way you'd misinterpret or fail to understand, God will begin by speaking to you through your Bible and through preachers that minister the Word.

God often relies on His earthly ministers to share with those incapable of hearing on their own. Perhaps you've been in church and have thought to yourself, "Now I don't know how he knew, but I needed to hear that today." How can that be? Your pastor isn't reading your mind, he's listening to the Spirit of the Lord, and the Holy Ghost is using him to touch your life. This is one reason why it is so important to be a part of a good local church, one that is preaching the Word of God.

The Word is the single most vital thing for the life of a believer. The Word gives God the opportunity to get through to you; it is a means of communication that is as active and alive as it was when the inspired individuals wrote it. If you don't put the Word in you, God can't give you revelation. He works through the Word! As you put the Word in you, God can begin to lead you by His Spirit.

You don't have to wait for a thundering voice or a vision to happen. When He lives in you, He'll guide and lead you, bringing you to revelation and to understanding through the written Word of God. If nothing fantastic ever happens in your life, if you never hear an audible voice in your whole life, it doesn't matter; just live by the Word.

Is it possible to be led by the Spirit even though you've not been baptized in the Holy Spirit as we discussed earlier in this chapter? Despite what many people think, yes. Remember, as a believer, the Spirit of God lives in you; He came into your life the day you were born again, and He can lead any Christian. But we must not dismiss the significance of being baptized in the Holy Spirit. It is an experience that is part of God's plan for the role of the Holy Spirit in your life. Once you understand all of the benefits of praying in tongues, you realize it's an added benefit that yields tremendous results!

God intends for the Holy Spirit to be your partner in life, leading you to victory every step of the way. He's your Helper, your Comforter, and the Spirit of Truth! But the level to which He can operate in your life depends on you allowing Him to. You can allow Him to sit dormant on the inside of you, or you can allow Him to have an active role by yielding your tongue to pray in the Spirit (tongues) and by following His leading in everything you do!

Key # 3

Living a Life of Faith

The next key to victorious living that we are going to talk about is living a life of faith. Now if you are someone who has been in church most of your life, you may think you've heard every message that could be taught on the subject. But let me encourage you—developing your faith is a continual process, and you must never grow weary in doing so. Faith is found throughout the Bible, from the beginning to the end, and you cannot live your life victoriously without it.

Faith Is the Victory

Let's begin this chapter in 1 John 5:4 where John writes, *"For whatever* [whoever] *is born of God overcomes the world. And this is the victory that has overcome the world— our faith"* (Comment added). As a believer, it is God's will for you to overcome the world! The word "world" here is referring to the world's system or the world's way of doing things, and you are to be above that. So, how do you overcome? Notice the latter part of that scripture, *"And this is the victory that has overcome the world—our faith."* In other words, "Faith is the victory that overcomes this world."

Notice what the Bible doesn't say. It doesn't say, "Love is the victory that overcomes this world." Now for some of you, a statement like that might challenge what you believe, so let me explain. Yes, Jesus gave us the commandment to love one another—that's very important, and we'll look at that in a later chapter—but you need to understand that love is how we are to relate with *people*. Faith is how you relate with *God*. And the only way you'll overcome in this world is by understanding how faith works in Him.

> **Faith is the victory that overcomes this world.**

You won't overcome the world with your mind. You won't overcome the world with your emotions. You won't overcome the world because you have managed to befriend everyone around you. Having faith in God is the only way you can do it.

How Faith Works

How does faith work? Let's look at salvation. In order to be born again you have to operate in faith (faith in Jesus). Notice Romans 10:9 says you are to *"confess with your mouth the Lord Jesus and believe in your heart."* That's how faith works!

For many believers, salvation is the end of their faith walk. They have faith in Jesus to be saved, but they continue to live their lives defeated by the same troubles and pitfalls people in the world do. They do not understand that God intends for them to be people of faith and that He intends for them to walk by faith every day.

Walk in Him

Hebrews 6:1,2 says that there are six basic doctrines in the Word of God. The one I want to focus on is faith toward God. As we've established, faith in Jesus is how you become born again, but faith toward God is your faith-walk in this life. It's how you are supposed to live your life every day.

When you were born again, you called upon the name of Jesus with confidence and absolute trust that you would spend eternity in Heaven with Him. Now, as a believer, that same confidence in God and that same assurance of victory in Him should be evident in your life, regardless of the circum-

> **And how do you get rooted and built up in Him? Through the Word.**

stances you face. You are to be steadfast in your belief that the Word of God is higher than what the world dictates to you. That's faith toward God.

Look at what the Apostle Paul writes in Colossians 2:5,6: *"For though I am absent in the flesh, yet I am with you in spirit, rejoicing to see your good order and the steadfastness of your faith in Christ. As you have therefore received Christ Jesus the Lord, so walk in Him."* Notice again what he says at the end—the same way you received Jesus as Lord is the same way you are to walk in Him.

So how do you walk in Him? Paul tells us in verse 7: by being *"rooted and built up in Him and established in the faith, as you have been taught, abounding in it with thanksgiving."* And how do you get rooted and built up in Him? Through the Word—your faith-walk is dependent on it (Romans 10:17).

Desire the Word

In 1 Peter 2:2, the Bible says, *"As newborn babes, desire the pure milk of the Word that you may grow thereby."* Just as a baby desires milk, we are to desire the Word. Think about that. How does a baby act? A baby wants milk, and he wants it now. He doesn't try to be polite about it. He just simply screams for it! Well, some of us need to get the same way about the Word of God. We need to be hungry for more of the Word; we need to desire His Word and feed our faith.

Without Faith, It's Impossible to Please Him

Notice the first part of Hebrews 11:6, where Paul writes, *"But without faith it is impossible to please Him."* In the Greek, the word used for "impossible" here means that you are "unable or disabled" to please God. In other words, without faith, you are unable to or disabled from pleasing God.

To comprehend the magnitude of this scripture for us today, you must understand that this wasn't written to those who were unsaved. This was written to believers—people who were born again. And the faith referred to in this scripture is not talking about faith for salvation; it's referring to faith toward God.

In essence, Paul is saying that if you try to live your life or face a situation relying on your own strengths and abilities instead of through faith in God and His Word, He is not pleased.

Your Faith Is Rewarded

Let's go back to Hebrews 11:6, but this time, we'll include the latter part of the scripture: "*But without faith it is impossible to please Him, for he who comes to God must believe that He is, and that He is a rewarder of those who diligently seek Him.*" The Greek literally says, "You must believe that God exists," and the word "reward" might more literally be translated, "payday." In other words, when you believe that God is, and you diligently seek Him, He will reward your faith!

How do you diligently seek God? Make sure you are in a local church being fed the Word of God on a regular basis, read your Bible daily, and take the time to get by yourself and pray. God will reward you. You'll begin to see things in the Word that you may not have noticed before. You'll gain a better understanding of what belongs to you as a child of God. You'll develop your faith!

Facing Opposition

Oftentimes, we don't understand the importance of living a life of faith until we face a situation and need to stand on the Word to overcome it. If opposition comes your way, and you've not developed your faith in that area—if you don't know and believe what God said in His Word about your circumstance or problem—then you'll have nothing on which to stand. You'll rely on your natural abilities because that's all you know. As a result, you'll struggle to overcome, and most likely your struggle will end in defeat.

On the other hand, if you are rooted in and built up on the Word, then you have strong faith. You'll believe in your heart and confess with your mouth what God has to say about your situation, and you'll walk right through it victoriously! That's faith in operation, and that pleases God!

Overcomers from the Old Testament

Hebrews 11—often referred to as the "faith chapter"—recalls the accounts of a number of Old Testament saints who overcame extraordinary circumstances through faith. Hebrews 11:33 tells us what these individuals of faith did in the face of opposition—they *"through faith subdued kingdoms, worked righteousness, obtained promises, stopped the mouths of lions."*

Daniel's victory in the lion's den is one mentioned here in Hebrews 11. The Bible tells us in Daniel chapter 6 that Daniel had been cast into the lion's den, and its entrance was sealed shut with a stone. The following morning, the king cried out to Daniel to see if he was still alive, and Daniel responded, *"My God sent His angel and shut the lions' mouths"* (Daniel 6:22).

Let's go on to Hebrews 11:34, where it mentions Shadrach, Meshach, and Abednego—the three Hebrew children who were thrown into the fiery furnace. The Bible tells us in Daniel chapter 3 that the flames of the furnace were so hot that those who were given the task of throwing the children in *died*, but the Hebrew children walked through the fire unharmed! The Bible says that their clothes didn't even smell like smoke, and their hair wasn't singed. And when the king looked in the furnace, he noticed a fourth man walking with the children when only three were thrown in. That fourth man was Jesus. How was that possible? Through faith. They put their faith in God and said, *"Our God whom we serve is able to deliver us from the burning fiery furnace, and He will deliver us from your hand, O King"* (Daniel 3:17).

> These individuals confessed that God would deliver them, and He did!

Are you beginning to see the incredible power of a life of faith? In the face of extreme opposition and almost certain death, these individuals confessed what they believed in their hearts to be true—that God would deliver them, and He did!

Faith Does Something

If you struggle in the area of faith because you know all of the mistakes you've made in life, let this be an encouragement to you. Abraham made many mistakes, and the Bible calls him the father of our faith (Romans 4:16).

In Genesis chapter 12, God told Abraham that He wanted him to *leave* his family and go. So what did Abraham do? He *took* his family and went. Did he obey the command of the Lord? Not exactly. He obeyed the "go" part, but ignored the part about leaving all of his family behind.

But do you know what God saw in Abraham? God saw a man who at least did something. He saw a man who was willing to obey and a man who was also willing to admit when he had made a mistake. If you can do that with God, He has a lot to work with.

Key # 4

Understanding Your Covenant Rights

So far, we have covered the first three keys to victorious living that we need to take hold of and utilize if we want victory in our lives. The first was receiving revelation knowledge from the Word. The second key was acknowledging the role of the Holy Spirit in our lives. We also looked at the third key, living a life of faith.

The fourth key we're going to cover is understanding your covenant rights in Christ.

Covenant Defined

Let me give you a definition of "covenant." A covenant is a type of contract, an agreement, which secures rights, benefits, and ramifications between two parties. Most likely you've entered into a contract or two in your lifetime. Maybe you've signed an agreement with a landlord to rent an apartment, or maybe you signed a contract to join a fitness center. Such agreements and contracts are a type of covenant, but they fall short of what the Bible would consider a true covenant. This is because such covenants are often broken in today's society. It's not uncommon for people to break their agreements and to even utilize lawyers to break contracts for them. Even the covenant of marriage has lost its significance in the eyes of many people, because too often it ends in divorce.

So let's look at what the Bible says about God and the covenants He makes to get a clear picture of what true covenant means. Deuteronomy 7:9 says, *"Therefore know that the Lord your God, He is God, the faithful God who keeps covenant and mercy for a thousand generations with those who love Him and keep His commandments."* God is faithful, and He keeps His covenants! He puts you in a binding agreement that He'll never break. That's true covenant.

The Old Covenant and the New Covenant

In the Word of God we find the Old Covenant, and the New Covenant. The names say it all—the old is just that, old—it has been replaced by a new and better covenant.

The Old Covenant was a foreshadowing of the New, and those who lived under it lived under the Levetical Law. Through the life, death, burial, and resurrection of Jesus, the Law was fulfilled, and the New Covenant was established.

God started His covenants, first of all, with Adam (Genesis chapter 2). But, Adam failed to keep his side of the covenant. As a result, the first relationship man had with God could not continue as it was. So God put His master plan of redemption into effect, while also making new, provisional agreements along the way. One such covenant agreement was with Noah (Genesis chapters 6-9), which saved his life and that of his family members. And later, God made a covenant with Abram, which is referred to as the Abrahamic Covenant (Genesis chapter 17).

When we read the account about Abram, we learn that when God made the covenant with him, He put him to sleep. Why? Because Abram didn't have anything to offer God.

The same is true of us. Romans 5:8 says that while you were yet a sinner, Christ died for you. You didn't make the covenant in which you live. When you are born again, all of the blessings of God are *freely given* to you. You don't have to work for them. They're all part of your covenant in Christ, the New Covenant.

For most of us, that's hard to imagine; it's a blow to our egos. And, depending on your background, you might have more trouble with that than others might. There's a part of each of us that wants to know we worked to get everything right with God. We want to feel that we're justified in receiving everything He has given us in our covenant. But the truth is we have nothing to offer but our lives and nothing to say except, "I accept you, Lord Jesus."

The New Covenant isn't dependent on our keeping the Law, as those under the Old Covenant were required to do. Yes, there are conditions for the New Covenant, but they are radically different from the Old.

As those who have called upon the Name of the Lord, Jesus, we can repent from the heart when we sin and move ahead with God. We don't have to wait for the yearly cleansing provided under the Old Covenant.

Understand, however, that doesn't mean that we should disregard the Old Covenant altogether. When viewed through the eyes of the New, the Old Covenant is beneficial in helping us understand our covenant rights in Christ, but it is no longer the standard by which we are judged.

New Identity

If you are familiar with the Old Testament, then you understand that there were all kinds of specific rituals involved with making covenant agreements in Abraham's day. Such rituals included cutting themselves and exchanging blood, exchanging coats, changing names, and exchanging tools. Each was highly symbolic of the exchange of benefits.

For example, when God made covenant with Abram, He changed Abram's name to Abraham and called him the father of many nations. Understand, Abraham was ninety-nine years of age at the time and did not have children. But through

> **We are now called the Church of the living God!**

covenant, God made him the father of many nations! In the same way, we were once scattered, but in our New Covenant through Christ we are a chosen generation, a royal priesthood, a holy nation (1 Peter 2:9). We are now called the Church of the living God!

It's in the Blood

In our covenant with God, He sees us through the blood of Jesus. The crown of thorns that pierced His brow, the lashes from the brutal whippings He endured, the spear that was driven into His side—all of these things took place so you could come into covenant with a God who wanted to be in covenant with you. Sin had a price, a just punishment, and it required the death of God's own perfect Son in our place. He was the perfect sacrifice—the Lamb of God.

Notice what Jesus said in 1 Corinthians 11:25 (NLT), *"This cup is the New Covenant between God and you, sealed by the shedding of my blood."* The blood that He shed at Calvary brought you into covenant with a great and mighty God who doesn't want anything from you other than relationship through His Son.

Heirs of the Promises

In Galatians 3:28,29 we read that under the New Covenant *"there is neither Jew nor Greek, there is neither slave nor free, there is neither male nor female; for you are all one in Christ Jesus."* In the Greek language it reads this way: "And if you be Christ's"—the Anointed One—"then you are Abraham's seed and an inheritor of the promise."

Now that we're born again, God looks at us and says that we can receive everything that God promised Abraham. So, what did God promise Abraham when He made covenant with him? He said that He would:

◆ Multiply Abraham exceedingly (Genesis 17:2)
◆ Make Abraham exceedingly fruitful (Genesis 17:6)
◆ Give Abraham and his descendents land (Genesis 17:8)

These are incredible promises that God made to Abraham, and because of our covenant rights through Christ, they're part of our inheritance!

Yes and Amen in Christ

Now, notice 2 Corinthians 1:20 (NIV), which says, *"For no matter how many promises God has made, they are all 'yes' in Christ. And so through Him the 'amen' is spoken by us to the glory of God."* As believers, if you find *any* promise in the Old Covenant made to an Old Covenant person, you can now take that promise as your own. The promises of God that belong to us are not limited to the promises God made with Abraham. They're *all* "yes" in Christ!

This is yet another reason why the Word of God is so vital—His promises are in the Word. If you want to know what belongs to you, you have to spend time in the Word. So let's go to the Word and find out some other promises that belong to us.

In Deuteronomy 28, God tells Moses about the blessings that will come upon those who observe His commands. Let's look at a few of them:

- *Blessed shall you be in the city, and blessed shall you be in the country* (Deuteronomy 28:3).
- *Blessed shall be the fruit of your body, the produce of your ground and the increase of your herds, the increase of your cattle and the offspring of your flocks* (Deuteronomy 28:4).
- *The Lord will cause your enemies who rise against you to be defeated before your face; they shall come out*

against you one way and flee before you seven ways (Deuteronomy 28:7).

♦ *The Lord will command the blessing on you in your storehouses and in all to which you set your hand, and He will bless you in the land which the Lord your God is giving you* (Deuteronomy 28:8).

♦ *The Lord will make you the head and not the tail; you shall be above only, and not beneath* (Deuteronomy 28:13).

And notice what David writes in Psalm 103:2-5:

Bless the Lord, O my soul, and forget not all His benefits: Who forgives all your iniquities, who heals all your diseases, who redeems your life from destruction, who crowns you with loving kindness and tender mercies, who satisfies your mouth with good things, so that your youth is renewed like the eagle's.

God is an awesome God! And His promises to those in covenant with Him bring abundant provision, great protection, and wondrous healing. Are you beginning to see the power of understanding your covenant rights? These promises of God belong to you! And it gets even better. Notice Hebrews 8:6,7 (NLT), which says,

But our High Priest has been given a ministry that is far superior to the ministry of those who serve under the old laws, for he is the one who guarantees for us a better covenant with God, based on better promises. If the first covenant had been faultless, there would have been no need for a second covenant to replace it.

Under the New Covenant in Christ, because we have a greater High Priest, Jesus, we have a better covenant based on *better promises*! Not only are we now recipients of all of the promises of God to those in the Old Testament, we are recipients of the promises of God in the New! So let's look at some of the promises of God under the New Covenant that they didn't have in the Old.

Benefits of the New Covenant

- **First** and foremost is the New Birth—being born again. Confessing Jesus as your Lord and Savior is a spiritual act without equal! (Romans 10:8-13)
- The **second** benefit is the habitation of God within us, which we discussed when we reviewed the second key to victorious living—understanding the role of the Holy Spirit. The same God that *came upon* the king and the priest and the prophet in the Old Covenant is the same God who *dwells* on the inside of *you*! (John 14:17, 1 Corinthians 6:15-20, 2 Corinthians 6:14-18)
- The **third** benefit is the baptism of the Holy Spirit with the evidence of speaking in other tongues. We have unprecedented access to the Holy Spirit in the New Covenant. Again, we touched on this earlier, but it's worth another look! In Luke 24:49, Jesus said, *"Behold, I send the Promise of my Father upon you: but tarry in the city of Jerusalem, until you are endued with power from on high."* That power from on high is the Holy Spirit, and in the original text the word for power used here is *dunamis,* which means "explosive power!"
- The **fourth** benefit of the New Covenant is that we become a new creation when we accept Christ. Second

Corinthians 5:17 says, *"Therefore, if anyone is in Christ, he is a new creation; old things have passed away; behold, all things have become new."* In the Greek language it says, "If any man be in Christ, he's a new species of being that never existed before." This doesn't mean that your outward appearance changes—you will still look the same—but on the inside, you become a *new* creation. When you are born again, you are born of God, and your very nature changes from that of a sinner to that of a child of God.

◆ The **fifth** benefit is the armor of God (Ephesians 6:10-18). In the Old Testament, the Israelites had God's protection, but there were times God's protection lifted. Under our covenant, God never pulls back on His side of the covenant. We never lose the *ability* to walk in His protec-

> He has provided us with His armor, and we activate that armor by being doers of the Word.

tion. Notice Ephesians 6:10,11, which says, *"Finally, my brethren, be strong in the Lord, and in the power of his might. Put on the whole armor of God, that you may be able to stand against the wiles of the devil."* God's protection is always available to us. He has provided us with His armor, and we *activate* that armor by being doers of the Word. When we choose not to obey the Word of God, *we* lay aside the protection He has provided.

◆ The **sixth** benefit is that we've been made righteous. Romans 3:21-24 tells us we are justified by the blood of Jesus and have been made righteous. Romans 3:20 (NLT) says, *"For no one can ever be made right in God's sight by doing what His Law commands. For the more we* *know God's Law, the clearer it becomes that we aren't obeying it."* Under the Old Covenant, the Israelites had no righteousness—only sins covered over by sacrifices. But, because of the blood of Jesus, we now have right standing with God!

◆ Number **seven** is that we become joint heirs with Christ. Romans 8:16,17 says, *"The Spirit Himself bears witness with our spirit that we are children of God. And if children, then heirs—heirs of God and joint heirs with Christ."* As a believer, you're an heir of God and joint heir with Jesus. Although we are not Jesus, we are co-equal with Him. The Greek literally says that you are coequal with Jesus. That is overwhelming! Understand, however, we are not Jesus, but He elevated us to a level together with Him.

◆ The **eighth** benefit is that we are seated in heavenly places in Christ. Ephesians 2:6 says that God, *"raised us up together, and made us sit together in the heavenly places in Christ Jesus."*

◆ Number **nine** is the blood of Jesus and the cleansing power that is in His blood. Forgiving power is in the blood. First John 1:7 says, *"But if we walk in the light as He is in the light, we have fellowship with one another, and the blood of Jesus Christ His Son, cleanses us from all sin."* The sacrifice of bulls and goats covered over their sins in the Old Covenant. But in the New Covenant, the blood of Jesus washes our sins away completely! (1 John 1:9, Ephesians 1:7)

◆ The **tenth** benefit is that under our covenant we are kings and priests. First Peter 2:9 says, *"But you are a chosen generation, a royal priesthood, a holy nation, His own special people."* The New Living Translation puts it this way: *"But you are not like that, for you are a chosen people. You are a kingdom of priests, God's holy nation."* There was a real spiritual hierarchy under the Old Covenant. There were Levitical priests, some prophets, and a handful of holy men, a few of which were kings. Everyone else just went to synagogue or to the temple and had very little in the way of a personal relationship with God. But for the New Covenant Christian, He makes each of us as priests! (Revelation 1:6)

- Number **eleven**: We are given authority to rule and reign on this earth. Romans 5:17 says, *"For if by one man's offense death reigned through one, much more those who receive abundance of grace and of the gift of righteousness will reign in life through the One, Jesus Christ."* Jesus has given us the ability to rule and reign on this earth. The devil might be the god of this world, but you are to rule and reign in life over him. For example, in Luke 10:19, we are promised that we can tread on serpents and scorpions. Serpents and scorpions represent the devil with his plans and schemes. You have the power to thwart his plans!

- The **twelfth** point is that we can approach God as individuals. Hebrews 4:16 says, *"Come boldly to the throne of grace, that we may obtain mercy and find grace to help in time of need."* God's throne is the throne of grace, not a throne of judgment. Under the New Covenant, each one of us has individual access to the presence of God!

- Number **thirteen** is that He has translated us into His kingdom. Colossians 1:13 (KJV) says, *"Who hath delivered us from the power of darkness, and hath translated us* *into the kingdom of his dear Son."* As New Covenant believers, we now walk in the light. God took you, spiritually speaking, and transferred you out of one kingdom into another. You live in the world, but you're not of it. (John 15:19; 17:14; 17:16)

◆ Number **fourteen** is that Jesus came to destroy the works of the devil, and under our covenant we enjoy that benefit! First John 3:8 (NLT) says that, *"the Son of God came to destroy these works of the devil."* The Greek literally says, "to render powerless or paralyze the works of the devil." The devil can't touch *your* life when you exercise your covenant rights with God! You have power over the enemy though Christ—resist the devil and he will flee from you. (James 4:7)

Exercise Your Rights

By accepting Christ into your heart, you partake of the greatest element of the New Covenant—being born again—as well as getting *all* of the promises of God old and new! We deserved nothing but death, yet God loved us so much that He made a way for us to spend eternity with Him. And through the New Covenant, sealed by the blood of Jesus, God provided us with everything we need to live a life of victory while on this earth.

Jesus gave His life for the covenant rights we have been given. Honor what He did on the cross—understand your covenant rights, and exercise them! Expect to live victoriously because you're in covenant with Almighty God!

Key # 5

A Renewed Mind

In the previous chapter, we discussed the fourth key for victorious living, which is understanding your covenant rights with God. Now it's time to move on to the fifth key, having a renewed mind. As a pastor, I have come to recognize that the process of renewing one's mind is a principle that many believers neglect. They have accepted Jesus into their hearts and are on their way to heaven, but they are not taking an active role in the renewal of their minds. How do I know this? It's apparent that the world influences them more than heaven does. They live their lives by what the world dictates to them instead of by the Word of God. And that's not God's way; that's not the way to victory!

It's important to understand that our behavior is a direct result of what we put into our minds. Some people think they can get away with feeding their minds garbage yet still expect to get something other than garbage out, but our behavior and thought process aren't going to change by themselves. Our minds must be renewed.

How Your Mind Is Renewed

You are a spirit, you live inside of a body, and you possess a mind. When you are born again, your spirit is made brand new, but your mind is not changed. Instead, your mind is in the process of being changed, or renewed. And unfortunately, there's no set amount of time necessary to renew your mind; it's a continual process, and it won't get total sanctification until Jesus returns.

James 1:21,22 says, *"Therefore lay aside all filthiness and overflow of wickedness, and receive with meekness the implanted Word, which is able to save your souls. But be doers of the Word, and not hearers only, deceiving yourselves."* In the Greek, the word "soul" could be translated "mind." Let's look at that Scripture again in that light: another way of saying it might be, "receive with meekness the engrafted Word, which is able to save your mind."

The word "receive" in the scripture above comes from a Greek word *lamabano*, which means "to take a hold of." The Word you receive, take a hold of, and allow to be implanted in your life is the thing that's going to renew your mind. And, the word "save" is the Greek word *sozo*, which means "to restore, to heal, to protect." The Word has the ability to restore, heal, and protect your mind! God knows our minds constantly need restored. And the only way to restore your mind is through His Word.

It's interesting to me that *we* are instructed to *receive* the Word, which is able to save our mind. I believe that no matter how good the message, a pastor can never implant the Word in your heart; hearing it from someone else will never change your mind unless you receive it. To plant the Word inside you, you need to receive it directly. The Word you *receive* and allow to be implanted on the inside of you is what will change you.

Most moral people have a hard time accepting that they have things inside them that need changing. However, for every year you live on earth, you have that many years of wrong influences to fight when you become a Christian. And it doesn't stop when you get saved; you must continually seek to have the Word implanted inside of you to renew your mind.

> The Word you receive is what will change you.

Learning God's Ways

When we talk about renewing the mind, we're talking about learning God's way of doing things. Notice the Amplified translation of Matthew 6:33, which says, *"But seek (aim at and strive after) first of all His kingdom and His righteousness (His way of doing and being right)."*

So in a sense, you could say that renewing your mind is replacing the worldly ways of doing things with God's ways. And God's ways are higher than our ways! This means that we love and forgive when the world has taught us to be angry and hold a grudge; this means we keep ourselves pure when the world has taught us to enjoy the moment; this means we must study and become acquainted with God's ways of doing things.

Living Sacrifice

Romans 12:1,2 is perhaps the most well-known scripture on renewing your mind. It says,

> *I beseech you therefore, brethren, by the mercies of God, that you present your bodies a living sacrifice, holy, acceptable to God, which is your reasonable service. And*

73

do not be conformed to this world, but be transformed by the renewing of your mind, that you may prove what is that good and acceptable and perfect will of God.

Part of renewing the mind is presenting your body as a living sacrifice to God. Why? Because your body houses your mind. And, if you're going to renew your mind properly, it's important to go to God on a regular basis and say, "God, I present my body a living sacrifice to you."

We renew our minds to replace *any* thought not in agreement with God's ways of doing things. It's our responsibility to replace whatever is not in accordance with His Word, not just extreme wrong conduct.

Ephesians 4:22-24 says,

Put off, concerning your former conduct, the old man which grows corrupt according to the deceitful lusts, and be renewed in the spirit of your mind, and that you put on the new man which was created according to God, in true righteousness and holiness.

Paul isn't just talking about fornication or murder; he's also talking about former conducts that seem far less serious, such as strife, gossiping, or stealing. Although seemingly small offenses, they are wrong in the eyes of God. They are actions motivated by your flesh.

When you combine your flesh's unredeemed desires with Satan's power to deceive, manipulate, and lie, you can be in real trouble! Paul spells out some examples of activities to deny your flesh of as he goes on in Ephesians 4:25-32 explaining what to do as you renew your mind:

Therefore, putting away lying, let each one of you speak truth with his neighbor, for we are members of one another. Be angry, and do not sin. Do not let the sun go down on your wrath, nor give place to the devil. Let him who stole steal no longer, but rather let him labor, working with his hands what is good, that he may have something to give him who has need. Let no corrupt word proceed out of your mouth, but what is good for necessary edification, that it may impart grace to the hearers. And do not grieve the Holy Spirit of God, by whom you were sealed for the day of redemption. Let all bitterness, wrath, anger, clamor, and evil speaking be put away from you, with all malice. And be kind to one another, tenderhearted, forgiving one another, just as God in Christ forgave you.

The mind-sets that your unsaved life has instilled in you will still be there when you get saved; it's up to you to receive the Word and renew your mind, in order to change your lifestyle.

The Battle of Our Flesh

Even some of the founders of the faith dealt with this issue; we're not the only ones. The Apostle Paul wrote in Romans 7:15-17 (NLT),

I don't understand myself at all, for I really want to do what is right, but I don't do it. Instead, I do the very thing I hate. I know perfectly well that what I am doing is wrong, and my bad conscience shows that I agree that the law is good. But I can't help myself, because it is sin inside me that makes me do these evil things.

He warred with his flesh to renew his mind. Notice verses 18-20 (NLT):

> *I know I am rotten through and through so far as my old sinful nature is concerned. No matter which way I turn, I can't make myself do right. I want to, but I can't. When I want to do good, I don't. And when I try not to do wrong, I do it anyway. But if I am doing what I don't want to do, I am not really the one doing it; the sin within me is doing it.*

It's the sin within us, the unredeemed mind, that causes us to fail to do right. But there's hope. Read on in verses 21-25:

> *It seems to be a fact of life that when I want to do what is right, I inevitably do what is wrong. I love God's law with all my heart. But there is another law at work within me that is at war with my mind. This law wins the fight and makes me a slave to the sin that is still within me. Oh, what a miserable person I am! Who will free me from this life that is dominated by sin? Thank God! The answer is in Jesus Christ our Lord. So you see how it is: In my mind I really want to obey God's law, but because of my sinful nature I am a slave to sin.*

Thank God! In Christ, we can walk in victory!

Be Not Conformed to This World

Romans 12: 2 says, "*And do not be conformed to this world.*" In this context, not being conformed to this world involves your attitudes. We're not to let the world form and shape our attitudes; it is possible for us to walk in this life and not conform to the world and its ways.

I've always found this interesting: the world conforms; the Word *transforms*. This word, "transformed," is *metemorphameo* in the Greek, from which we get our word "metamorphosis." Metamorphosis is simply this—the process of change. Most of us are familiar with the process of change by which a caterpillar becomes a butterfly; in fact, many people make that immediate association with the word metamorphosis.

Caterpillars spin a cocoon, and they undergo a process where, if you open up the cocoon, it is pretty ugly. There are all kinds of things taking place in there, and there's a reason why it's hidden—it's ugly! When you're renewing your mind, some things are going to get ugly. When you begin to renew your mind, and the light of the Word begins to shine on your attitudes, behaviors, and ideas, you see how truly ugly they are.

The process of change doesn't happen overnight. But after you've been saved a while, you should be able to see a noticeable change in the way you conduct yourself.

So don't be conformed to the world, but instead put your mind through the process of renewal with the Word of God. That word "renew" is a Greek word meaning "to renovate or to remodel." Your mind needs change; you need to renovate your lifestyle, but only you can put the Word into action to change it.

If you've ever watched a renovation process in a house, you know it can—and will—get messy. Before renovation it looked okay, but during renovation it will get ugly. Dust and dirt gets everywhere, but in the process, the old things are changed into something new and beautiful.

The renewal process in your mind might start innocently enough with the kitchen, but if you've ever remodeled, you know that once you start, it begins a chain reaction, and you begin to notice that everything needs to be renovated. You thought you just had one area to work on but quickly discover there are all kinds of areas in your life that need work. Your new kitchen will show you how ugly the bathroom is, or the den, or whatever—they all symbolize areas in your thought life, your attitudes, and your behaviors. It might be the individuals you need to love or forgive; it might be behavior. Whatever the case, the important thing is to embrace the needed changes.

Spiritual Renovations

Here's a tip: you can't try to help others in the renewal process of their minds. God does not renew everyone in the same area at the same time, and you can't hold others in condemnation for things that God has renewed within you—or is in the process of renewing. When someone says something that hits home and irritates you, it's usually because your pride is reacting to something that the Holy Spirit has been convicting you of where you haven't yet been renewed. You know what they're saying is right, but you don't want to admit it. Knowing you can trigger that pride in someone else should make you careful what you share and how you share it. Renewal of others is God's job, not ours.

The first two keys we discussed, revelation and being led by the Spirit, are both very important in the process of renewing your mind. Revelation of the Word is what gets the Word inside of you, renewing you; and listening to the Spirit is what helps you to be led by the Word instead of being led by the world. Be certain that you are constantly trans-forming your mind through the Word. If you are not transformed by the renewing of your mind to the Word, you will be conformed to the world. There is no such thing as standing still in God. You're either progressing or you're falling away by conforming to the world. The renewal process requires abandoning your worldly ways and doing things God's way.

> The renewal process requires abandoning your worldly ways and doing things God's way.

Key # 6

Forgiveness

The sixth key I want to present to you is that of forgiveness. We'll see how unforgiveness will prevent your faith from operating, and how it can seriously hamper your ability to have victory in your life.

It would be nice if people never did anything for which you had to forgive them, but they will. And, most likely, someone has to forgive you for things you've done. Very rarely do people do things intentionally to hurt you, just as you rarely do things to hurt others. But we all will do things for which we need to be forgiven, and others will do things that we have to forgive.

All of Us Are Required to Forgive

You will never find a successful, faith-filled believer who harbors unforgiveness in his or her heart. Why? Because you can't live in victory with unforgiveness in your life.

In every situation, regardless of circumstances, we are required to forgive. A prime example is Stephen, who we read about in Acts 7:59,60 (NLT): *"And as they stoned him, Stephen prayed, 'Lord Jesus, receive my spirit.' And he fell to his knees, shouting, 'Lord, don't charge them with this sin!' And with that, he died."* Stephen is being stoned, but while he's being stoned, he asks the Lord to forgive those who were stoning him to death! He's doing the exact same thing Jesus did while hanging on the cross. Notice Luke 23:34, which says, *"Then Jesus said, 'Father, forgive them, for they do not know what they do.' "* Both of these are incredible examples from the Bible on forgiveness.

> You will never find a successful, faith-filled believer who harbors unforgiveness.

Most likely, you've not had someone treat you as Stephen and Jesus were treated. Sometimes we think our own wounds are close to being this bad, but the reality is that Jesus was being crucified and Stephen was being repeatedly beaten with large, bone-breaking rocks. And yet they both had the ability and desire to forgive, and it didn't take them months to do so; they forgave people right in the midst of it all. How? They understood the importance of forgiveness, and the critical connection between forgiveness and faith.

Faith is how you receive what you need from God. Without a lifestyle of forgiveness, you'll never receive what you need from God. Notice what Jesus says in Mark 11:22-26:

So Jesus answered and said to them, "Have faith in God. For assuredly, I say to you, whoever says to this mountain, 'Be removed and be cast into the sea,' and does not doubt in his heart, but believes that those things he says will be done, he will have whatever he says. Therefore I say to you, whatever things you ask when you pray, believe that you receive them, and you will have them. And whenever you stand praying, if you have anything against anyone, forgive him, that your Father in heaven may also forgive you your trespasses. But if you do not forgive, neither will your Father in heaven forgive your trespasses."

Jesus is telling us we can have the "faith of God." We can move mountains! But notice verse 25, which says, *"And when you stand praying, if you have anything against anyone, forgive him."* Our faith is tied to forgiveness. If we fail to forgive, our faith is hindered and those mountains we want moved out of our way will loom before us until we can get our hearts right and forgive.

> **If you want to keep your faith powerful, you must forgive.**

When we're dealing with unforgiveness, we can still wear the mask on the outside and make all the right expressions. We can even fool ourselves sometimes; but God is not deceived. He sees the heart.

If you want to keep your faith powerful, you must forgive. We need to be quick to ask God to forgive us if we've sinned, and quick to forgive others if they've done something to us. Wouldn't you want the same thing in return? Even the world knows this; they call it the Golden

Rule. But as believers, it's of even greater importance that we forgive quickly because the longer we harbor unforgiveness, the longer our faith is quenched. When you get a revelation about that fact, you'll realize that no hurt, or offense, is worth having your faith deactivated!

Many people have faith, yet their faith just isn't working because of unforgiveness. They've put the Word in, they meditate on it, but they're holding on to unforgiveness, and as a result, their faith is rendered powerless.

Why We Fail to Forgive

Did you know that the opposite of faith is fear? I believe that unforgiveness is often motivated by fear. And who is the author of fear and deceit? The devil. So guess who is trying to keep your faith down by making you afraid to forgive? That's right, the devil. And, if you're not in faith, you open the door to the devil to make a mess of things in your life. Why would people be afraid to forgive? Let's look at two reasons:

The **first** reason many people don't forgive is that they're afraid the person will do it to them again. They're afraid that it will give that other person a license to hurt them as often as they want to, and they don't want to go through it another time.

The Bible tells us that where there is fear, there is torment. And fear opens the doors for the very evil things you're afraid of to enter your life. If you're afraid that the person is going to hurt you again, *you are* opening the door for them to do it to you again! So what does forgiveness entail? It means that you're unafraid of them—that you've cast that burden, that fear, onto God and that you are trusting Him that He'll protect you so that you can forgive them.

Bullinger's Greek Lexicon of Words translates the word "forgiveness," as, "to treat the guilty party as though they've never sinned, or to treat them as innocent." Treating someone as innocent means treating them as though they didn't do it in the first place.

Don't get me wrong: all of your feelings will probably tell you that forgiving them and treating them as though they didn't do what they did is stupid and frightening. But we have to go by the Word, not by our feelings.

The **second** reason people are afraid to forgive is that we often feel that we are responsible for making the person pay a price for hurting us. We want to put them in the penalty box for a while. Many husbands and wives spend a lot of time in the penalty box or the doghouse— whatever you want to call that place of isolation and punishment. We want them to have to wait and work their way out.

But Jesus never said that. Regardless of the sin that someone might do against you, Jesus said, "Forgive them." He didn't make any allowance for the size of the infraction and the time period in which you have before you have to forgive them. I am glad that I didn't have to put in any time in the penalty box when I called on the name of the Lord to be saved. God doesn't put you in the penalty box, and that's not how you are to operate if you want to live a victorious life.

Ephesians 4:31,32 says, *"Let all bitterness, wrath, anger, clamor, and evil speaking be put away from you, with all malice. And be kind to one another, tenderhearted, forgiving one another, just as God in Christ forgave you."* Pay special attention to that last part—we're to forgive one another even as God in Christ has forgiven us. This caution against bitterness is echoed in Hebrews 12:14,15, which says, *"Pursue peace with all people, and holiness, without which no one will see the Lord: looking carefully lest anyone fall short of the grace of God; lest any root of bitterness, springing up, cause trouble, and by this many become defiled."*

The New Living Translation says,

> *Try to live in peace with everyone, and seek to live a clean and holy life, for those who are not holy will not see the Lord. Look after each other so that none of you will miss out on the special favor of God. Watch out that no bitter root of unbelief rises up among you, for whenever it springs up, many are corrupted by its poison.*

Bitterness comes from unforgiveness; it's pretty simple. It germinates in you like a seed. Bitterness sprouts or "springs up" and it will trouble you. In the Greek, instead of "trouble" it says, "It will crowd you." It will crowd you, annoy you, and harass you.

A Life of Forgiveness

Forgiveness is a lifestyle just as surely as entertaining fear or faith is a lifestyle. When you are in unforgiveness, something happens to you. For example, if someone does something to you, at first you may be able to resist the urge to run around telling everyone what he did to you. Yet you stew over it because you've not done anything to get rid of it. It just festers in you. Eventually, someone comes up to you and says, "Remember so-and-so?

Did you hear what he did to me?" They tell you all about what so-and-so did and you begin to think, "I knew it. This person does that to everybody, not just me!" And then that unforgiveness that you left unresolved in your heart explodes and grows inside of you.

As you stew over what happened to you instead of forgiving, that bitterness and unforgiveness takes root, and those roots spread out and crush your faith. Suddenly, you can't use your faith. And it doesn't stop there. Others come along and water your unforgiveness by what they say. The offense gets watered and grows, and that process continues until you cut off the supply that's feeding it by forgiving.

Pushing it down isn't the same as forgiving. You can try to forget and to move on, but you must forgive. Otherwise it's like a volcano, and eventually the bitterness will erupt in your life.

So that begs the question, "What do I do about it?" Maybe this is where you're living right now, or have been in the past, but you can build your faith back up simply by removing the issues in your life that tear it down. First of all, letting someone else in on your troubles with so-and-so is not the answer; in fact, they will just add to the weights pulling your faith down.

Faith to Forgive

Matthew 18:21,22 says, *"Then Peter came to Him and said, 'Lord, how often shall my brother sin against me, and I forgive him? Up to seven times?' Jesus said to him, 'I do not say to you, up to seven times, but up to seventy times seven.'"* How did the apostles respond to what Jesus said? Notice

Luke 17:5, "(Lord) *increase our faith.*" Now the Word says that of faith, hope, and love, the greatest is love, but the disciples didn't ask for love in order to deal with this command Jesus gave them regarding forgiveness. Why? Because it takes faith to forgive someone.

Even though the disciples asked Jesus to increase their faith to forgive, the Word teaches us that faith comes one way—faith comes by hearing, and hearing by the Word of God (Romans 10:17).

You have to build your faith to forgive by reading and confessing the Word. You have to have the mind-set, "This is what the Bible says about forgiveness, so this is what I'm going to do." Confess the Word and build your faith!

Remember, Jesus told Peter to forgive even if it's 490 times a day! That's once every few minutes of the day if you factor in hours for sleeping. In Luke, He tells the apostles that we have to forgive even if someone sins against us seven times a day and repents.

This scripture goes on into a story Jesus tells of a king with many servants; one of whom owes the king a significant amount of money—the equivalent of millions of dollars. When the accounts were called due, this servant couldn't pay his master, and the king commanded that he be thrown into prison. Everything he owned, including his wife and children, was to be sold to pay

> **You have to build your faith to forgive by reading and confessing the Word.**

off the debt. The servant begged for mercy, and the king forgave him his debt. However, that same servant, having just been forgiven, demanded that another servant pay him the comparatively small debt he owed him. This other servant also begged for time to pay the debt, but the servant forgiven the millions in debt didn't have mercy on his fellow servant and had him thrown in jail. When the king heard what this unforgiving servant did, he was angry and sentenced him to be tortured until he could pay his debt.

Matthew 18:35 (NLT) ends the passage by saying, *"That's what my heavenly Father will do to you if you refuse to forgive your brothers and sisters in your heart."* That's a rather extreme example, but it is a good analogy. The petty, small things that others do to us often pale in comparison to our sins against God for which He has forgiven us.

Forgive As You Are Forgiven

If you listen to some people, you'll hear the root of bitterness poisoning their lives and hurting their faith. If you're still talking about a past hurt or offense, it's a sure sign you haven't let it go yet. True biblical forgiveness is to treat the guilty party as though they never sinned against you.

Just as the wicked servant couldn't pay back his millions of dollars in debt, we are unable to pay the price our sinful nature demands. That's why Jesus paid it for us. When we try to make others pay for what they've done to us, we've failed to understand that it doesn't work that way. They can never pay.

Jesus paints a very familiar picture of our behavior with His example; we often hold things against people, but these sins against us are nothing compared to those we've committed against God and that He has forgiven.

If God treated us as we so often treat others, we wouldn't know what to do! He'd say, "Now that's a dozen times you've committed this sin since you've been saved. Enough! That's it; I've had it!"

Some people have that image of God, but that's not what the Bible reveals about Him. He is full of grace and mercy. Remember, His mercies are new every morning.

Forgiveness takes faith, but unforgiveness *damages* our faith. God forgave us our incalculable debt. We walk away totally forgiven when we accept His Son as our Savior! And then we can find the faith to say, "Father, forgive them. Don't count this sin against them." Don't let bitterness take hold in your heart; forgive quickly and allow your faith to generate victory in your life.

Key # 7

Walking in Love

In this chapter, we'll be covering the seventh key to victorious living. In the last chapter, we discussed forgiveness and how important it is to be forgiving if you want your faith to work. Now we are going to cover walking in love and the critical role it plays in your ability to live a life of victory.

Most of us know John 3:16: *"For God so loved the world that He gave His only begotten Son, that whoever believes in Him should not perish but have everlasting life."*

Now notice Romans 5:8, which says, *"But God demonstrates His own love toward us, in that while we were still sinners, Christ died for us."* The Greek says, "But God introduced His love towards us." God introduced His love to you and me when Jesus died on that cross.

> **God has put His love in us so that we can love others.**

Here's what I have found out about walking in love and the message of love: you can't love someone properly until you learn how God loves you. Until you understand that—until you receive revelation on it from Him—you won't be able to love others as you should. God has to put His love in us so that we *can* love others with His unconditional love.

God's Style of Love

Human love is selfish; God's is not. God's love is unconditional toward you, and it's different from any type of human love. If we aren't full of God's love and don't understand it, we won't be able to share it with others.

The word "love" in both of the scriptures we've looked at is the same. It's the Greek word *agape*. Many of the places in the Bible where the word "love" is used, it appears as either *agape* or *agapio*. They're two different words both dealing with the kind of love that God has for you. It's unconditional—not expecting anything in return.

Human love's not like that. Human love always expects something in return. If you want to learn about the difference between human love and God's love, observe how it works with your friends and your family. We'll always expect something in return until we begin to understand God's style of loving. Romans 5:5 says, *"The love of God has been poured out in our hearts by the Holy Spirit who was given to us."* You have to put in time studying the Word and perfecting your understanding of it in order to truly do as you're commanded. Love, just like faith, must be exercised. We think that just because we got saved, we're automatically going to be able to love in God's way. It doesn't work that way; you have to practice, and it doesn't come naturally to an unrenewed mind. The only way to love as God does is to get a revelation of what already resides in you. The only way we'll ever be able to love as He does is to have Him active in our lives, as we build our faith and our knowledge of the Word and His ways.

All of Us Are Required to Walk in Love

Notice what Paul writes in Ephesians 5:1,2: *"Therefore be imitators of God as dear children. And walk in love, as Christ also has loved us and given Himself for us, an offering and a sacrifice to God for a sweet-smelling aroma."* Walking in love is when we walk the way Jesus would in a situation even when we would prefer to do something else. Failing to walk in love is when we do something that we know is different from what Jesus and the Word tells us to do.

John 13:34,35 says, *"A new commandment I give to you, that you love one another; as I have loved you, that you also love one another. By this all will know that you are My disciples, if you have love for one another."* But loving one another doesn't just include other Christians or people that are nice to you. In Matthew 5:44, Jesus even tells us to love our enemies.

God gives only two commandments in the New Testament. First John 3:22,23 says,

And whatever we ask we receive from Him, because we keep His commandments and do those things that are pleasing in His sight. And this is His commandment: **that we should believe on the name of His Son Jesus Christ and love one another,** *as He gave us commandment.* (Emphasis added)

These are our two commandments under the New Covenant—believe in Jesus and love one another. And loving one another is not only a command, it's how we show we love God.

First John 2:5 says, *"But whoever keeps His word, truly the love of God is perfected in him. By this we know that we are in Him."* The next verse goes on to say, *"He who says he abides in Him ought himself also to walk just as He walked."* How did Jesus walk, and how are we supposed to walk? In love.

You can perfect the love of God that's inside you by being a doer of the Word. This is especially true when we obey the Word and do something such as loving even when it's a struggle and we don't want to do so. God's love is being perfected in you when you can have *agape* love even for those who are unlovely and who do not treat you right.

Walking in Love and Your Faith

Galatians 5:6 says, *"For in Christ Jesus neither circumcision nor uncircumcision avails anything, but faith working through love."* Therefore, we know when we get born again, immediately our faith is energized because the love of God is shed abroad in our heart. How can we keep our faith energized? By being doers of the Word. When we covered the sixth key to victorious living, forgiveness, we learned that to keep our faith powerful we must forgive. The same is true of our love walk. If we want to keep our faith energized, we have to walk in love as Jesus commanded. Look at 1 John 3:22 again, but this time I want to focus on the first part of the scripture: "*And whatever we ask we receive from Him, because we keep His commandments and do those things that are pleasing in His sight.*" When we walk in love with one another, we are keeping the commandment Jesus gave us. Then we can ask and receive!

Love: the New Testament Commandment

Walking in love can often seem very difficult. First John 2:7-11 (NLT), however, simplifies it by reducing it to one commandment:

Dear friends, I am not writing a new commandment, for it is an old one you have always had, right from the beginning. This commandment—to love one another—is the same message you heard before. Yet it is also new. This commandment is true in Christ and is true among you, because the darkness is disappearing and the true light is already shining. If anyone says, "I am living in the light," but hates a Christian brother or sister, that person is still living in darkness. Anyone who loves other Christians is living in the light and does not cause anyone to stumble. Anyone who hates a Christian brother or sister is living and walking in darkness. Such a person is lost, having been blinded by the darkness.

Most of us can readily say we don't hate anyone, but it's important that we recognize that in this day and age, the word "hate" is often replaced with phrases such as, "I sure dislike so-and-so," or "I'm not fond of so-and-so." We dislike what they do, or we don't appreciate something they say, and we think that's okay because surely we don't *hate* them. But, the original text for this word "hate" in 1 John means, "to have active feelings of ill will toward a brother or sister in word or in deed." This can be people that you just don't like; it's anyone that you'd treat with anything less than *agape* love.

And this is a passage with a promise: if you love your brother and sister, you'll be in the light, you won't stumble, and you won't make others to stumble by doing things for which they need to forgive you.

Here's another interesting detail about this verse: the darkness and blindness that it talks about isn't in your natural eyes. It's talking about the eyes of your understanding. My eyes that see spiritually are blinded when I hate or have active feelings of ill will towards another brother or sister!

Love and Forgiveness

When the eyes of your understanding are blind and unable to receive revelation, you'll find that when a preacher is teaching on something that others are receiving as revelation, you're blinded to it; when you're reading the Word, it will often seem like just a dry, dead book you read by discipline.

None of us wants to be in that condition. We want our eyes open, spiritually speaking. We want to be able to see. We want to be able to grow in the Lord.

This is where forgiveness ties in. When you have failed to love, it's time to forgive and restore light to your eyes. This type of behavior—loving people with *agape* love and forgiving those who have hurt us and caused us to fail in loving them—shows how God's

> **When you have failed to love, it's time to forgive.**

love is perfected in us. First John 4:7 says, *"Beloved, let us love one another, for love is of God; and everyone who loves is born of God and knows God."* God *is* love! But we won't love as He does simply because we are born again. We have to develop the love of God that lives inside of us.

Love, along with joy and others, is a fruit of the Spirit. And all of the fruit grows and develops in our lives over time as we mature; it doesn't just happen overnight. First John 4:8-11 goes on to say,

> *He who does not love does not know God, for God is love. In this the love of God was manifested toward us, that God has sent His only begotten Son into the world, that we might live through Him. In this is love, not that we loved God, but that He loved us and sent His Son to be the propitiation for our sins. Beloved, if God so loved us, we also ought to love one another.*

Perfecting His Love in You

So how do you perfect the love of God in you? Become a doer of the Word, and practice loving—even when you really don't want to love. This is crucifying your flesh.

The Bible tells us it's easy to love those who love you, and it's true. It's easy to love those who haven't hurt or offended us. So it's easy to be a doer of the Word when it involves people and situations that are easy to deal with; it's easy to practice and perfect God's love in you when you're dealing with people you love and who love you.

But here's where you begin to grow: when you present yourself to God as a living sacrifice, crucifying your flesh in order to practice the Word even when you don't want to—even when it's hard to love. We need to be mature enough to deal with people and events with God's love. He will give you grace to love through your situation.

In Closing

I've read many books in my lifetime and have heard many great sermons. You probably have done the same, and would probably agree that they are important to your walk with God. That is why I believe this book is one that will help you grow closer to God when you read it today and hopefully again and again. However, it is extremely important that you understand that no book or sermon will help you unless you apply the truths of the Word of God to your life.

- Seek revelation knowledge from the Word and in prayer.
- Be sensitive to the leading of the Holy Spirit and pray in the Spirit.
- Develop strong faith—know and believe what the Word says about you, and about the circumstances or situations you are facing.
- Exercise your covenant rights and remember that the promises of God are "yes" and "amen" to those in Christ.
- Renew your mind with the Word.
- Be quick to forgive.
- And always and at all times walk in love.

When you apply these principles in your life and begin to walk in them, you'll find that victory is no longer out of reach but is in every step you take in God!

Keep the Word before you. Live your life by the Word. Remind yourself of what God has done for you in Christ, and walk in victory until Jesus returns. Utilize your keys to victorious living!

"How Do I Get to Heaven?"

The Bible declares that we can know that we have eternal life. First John 5:13 reads, *"These things have I written unto you that believe on the name of the Son of God; that ye may know that ye have eternal life, and that ye may believe on the name of the Son of God."*

Acts 2:21 tells us that, *"...whosoever shall call on the name of the Lord shall be saved."* And Romans 10:9,10 (NKJV) reads, *"That if you confess with your mouth the Lord Jesus, and believe in your heart that God has raised Him from the dead, you will be saved. For with the heart one believes to righteousness; and with the mouth confession is made to salvation."*

Laying hold on eternal life is as simple as believing that Jesus Christ is the Son of God, that He died and was raised from the dead, and then confessing (or saying) that with your mouth. If you have never called on the Name of the Lord—don't put it off one more day. The following is a prayer of salvation. Read aloud this prayer and receive eternal salvation!

Prayer of Salvation

"Heavenly Father, I come to you in Jesus' Name. The Bible says that if I call on the name of the Lord, I will be saved. So, I do that now. I believe in my heart that Jesus came to the earth, was crucified, and rose from the dead. I confess that Jesus is Lord. I thank you that I am now a Christian—a child of God! I am saved and have received eternal life."

If you just prayed this prayer out loud, the Bible says you have instantly become a new creature in Christ: *"old things have passed away, behold all things are new"* (2 Corinthians 5:17). You will never be the same. Now you need to find a good local church and get involved as part of the family of God. Find a church that will love and care for you, and teach you the Word of God.

Michael Cameneti
Additional teachings from *this author*
To Order: Visit our website at **www.ccfchurch.com** or call **1-888-872-4991**.

Healing Made Simple
Pastor Michael Cameneti

It is God's will for His people to walk in divine health every day of their lives; He has promised healing in His Word. In this book, you'll learn where sickness comes from, the benefits included in God's plan of redemption, and the power of Christ in you. With powerful revelation from the Word of God and straight-forward delivery, Pastor Mike imparts "Healing Made Simple."

Paperback **\$12⁰⁰** #336-01

Home Improvement
Pastor Michael Cameneti

Statistics show that in the world today, 50% of marriages end in divorce. With this staggering figure, we need to examine the blueprint for building and maintaining a strong marriage and family. In this series, Pastor Michael Cameneti examines the basic building blocks needed for structuring a solid family and home.

8-tape audio series **\$32⁰⁰** #1144

Winning the Battle of the Mind
Pastor Michael Cameneti

It has been said that all faith battles are either won or lost in the mind. You will learn how you can renew your mind so that your spirit will dominate you in this life! There is a way to complete victory by putting off the old thoughts and putting on the new.

7-tape audio series **\$28⁰⁰** #1149

Having the Spirit of Faith
Pastor Michael Cameneti

Every day, we have opportunity after opportunity to allow what we see and what we feel to affect us. But, as Christians, such things should not cause us to waver; we are to live by faith – faith that is based on the truth of the Word of God. Faith believes that nothing is impossible with God. Faith speaks the Word to life's situations and determines to believe God's report over any other.

6-tape audio series **\$24⁰⁰** #1166

About Canton Christian Fellowship™

A Church to Call Home™

Pastors Michael &
Barbara Cameneti

Pastors Mike and Barb Cameneti, under the direction of the Holy Spirit, established Canton Christian Fellowship in the winter of 1988. Today, CCF has grown into a large, diverse, and multifaceted ministry, impacting people of all ages in our community and beyond. Sensitive to the leading of the Holy Spirit, Pastors Mike and Barb boldly minister the uncompromised Word of God clearly and accurately, with the gifts of the Spirit accompanying the preaching of the Word.

It is our desire to provide an environment where you and your family will experience the goodness of God and His abounding love toward you. If you do not have a home church and live in the Canton area, we invite you to be a part of our church family. At Canton Christian Fellowship, we're "A Church to Call Home."

Pastor Mike can also be seen on our *Keys to Victorious Living*™ television broadcast every week. Check our website for program listings.

Keys to
Victorious
Living™

Contact Information:
PO Box 35309 • Canton, Ohio 44735
www.ccfchurch.com • 330-492-0925